Axum: The History and Legacy of the Kingdom of Aksum's Capital and One of the Oldest Continuously Inhabited Cities in Africa

By Charles River Editors

Bair's picture of the tallest obelisk in Axum

About Charles River Editors

Charles River Editors provides superior editing and original writing services across the digital publishing industry, with the expertise to create digital content for publishers across a vast range of subject matter. In addition to providing original digital content for third party publishers, we also republish civilization's greatest literary works, bringing them to new generations of readers via ebooks.

Sign up here to receive updates about free books as we publish them, and visit Our Kindle Author Page to browse today's free promotions and our most recently published Kindle titles.

Introduction

Z. Helm's picture of stelae at Axum

Axum

"The Tigreans had Axum, but what could that mean to the Gurague? The Agew had Lalibela, but what could that mean to the Oromo? The Gonderes had castles, but what could that mean to the Wolaitai?" - Ethiopian Prime Minister Meles Zenawi, in response to a question about Ethiopian unity

In the year 570 CE, a child by the name of Muhammad is born in the Arabian city of Mecca. Sixty-two years later, he dies, and upon his death, the faith that he founded, Islam ("obedience to the one God"), dominates the western half of the Arabian Peninsula. By the end of the first millennium CE, four centuries after the death of Muhammad, Islam has grown to dominate western Asia, north and east Africa, the Levant, and the Iberian Peninsula.

The Holy Lands are lost to Christianity, and Christian Europe is under siege. Folk tales begin to circulate — their origins obscure, but first noted in historic texts around the 12th century CE — of a lost Christian kingdom in the East, the Kingdom of Prester John. There resides the patriarch of Saint Thomas, who proselytized in the Orient. Later, in the 15th century, under the impetus of the Portuguese King Henry the Navigator, Portuguese missionaries and navigators enter the Indian Ocean from the south and, creeping northward up the east coast of Africa, hear ever more substantial tales of a Christian kingdom lost in the belly of Islam. As they enter upon the coast of Somalia, competing in a growing trade in slaves and gold with Arabs of the peninsula, they become increasingly interested in the source of this legend, in part to fulfil the centuries-long dream of discovering the Kingdom of Prester John, but also in part to secure the alliance of a Christian power against the force of Islam.

In 1515, a Portuguese missionary explorer by the name of Father Francisco Álvares enters Ethiopia and takes note in the interior of the remnants of a civilization of obviously Christian origin, with living adherents conforming to a branch of the faith clearly founded in deepest antiquity. Could this be the Kingdom of Prester John? Father Álvares is intrigued, but wary of too fanciful a construction, and he speculates more practically on the legend of King Solomon, the Queen of Sheba, and other such muses. The city at the center of the civilization he calls *Aquasumo*.

Thus the existence of the Kingdom of Aksum came to the notice of Christian Europe after almost a millennium of isolation. The Portuguese had their own motivations for reaching and taking note of African antiquity, but as has often been true of the Portuguese relationship with Africa, their earliest explorations tended to be eclipsed by the work of later European explorers representing the wealthier nations of Europe.

Axum: The History and Legacy of the Kingdom of Aksum's Capital and One of the Oldest Continuously Inhabited Cities in Africa examines the amazing history and legacy of one of the most interesting places in the world. Along with pictures of important people, places, and events, you will learn about Axum like never before.

Axum: The History and Legacy of the Kingdom of Aksum's Capital and One of the Oldest Continuously Inhabited Cities in Africa

About Charles River Editors

Introduction

   Aksum in the Ancient World

   The Emergence of Aksum

   Architecture and Other Expressions of Civilization and Culture

   Kingship and Government

   Trade and Coinage

   Religion

   The Decline of the Kingdom

   Online Resources

   Further Reading

Free Books by Charles River Editors

Discounted Books by Charles River Editors

Aksum in the Ancient World

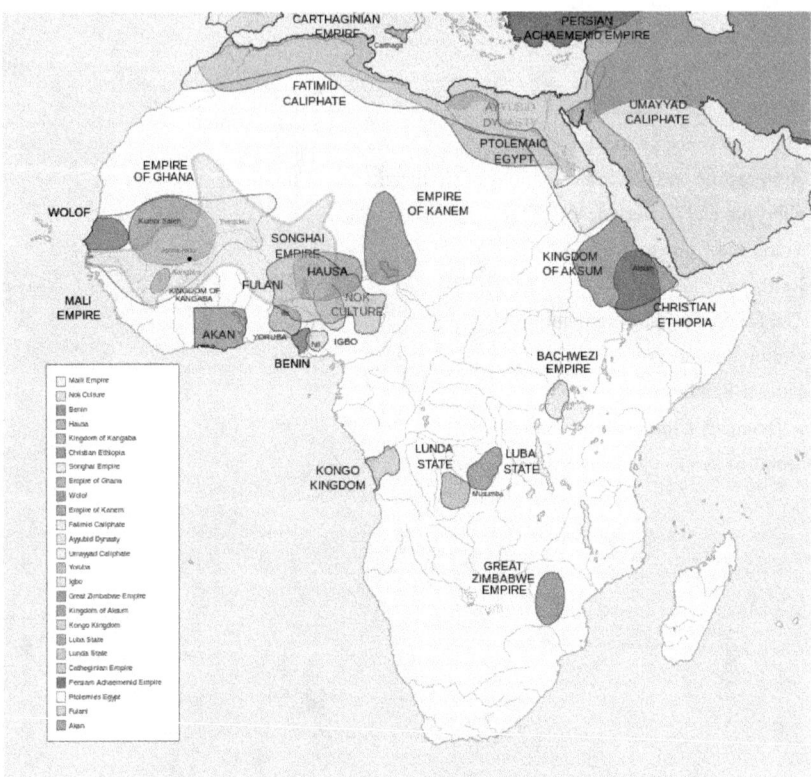

Jeff Israel's map of African kingdoms from 100-900 CE

When the Portuguese entered the interior of Africa, their quest was less about the discovery of the Kingdom of Prester John than the search for the source of the Nile, which emerged in the late 18th and early 19th centuries as something of a geographic Holy Grail. The source of the White Nile was not categorically confirmed until 1875-1876, when Welsh-American explorer Henry Morton Stanley circumnavigated Lake Victoria Nyanza, confirming an earlier theory put forward by John Hanning Speak that the principal outflow from this lake marked the commencement of the White Nile.

Stanley

The White Nile debate was ugly, divisive, and controversial, and it lingered in the geographic memory of Europe for a long time. The Blue Nile, on the other hand, which confluences with the White Nile at Khartoum, the capital of Sudan, was relatively quickly and accurately determined to rise out of the Ethiopian Highlands. Lake Tana, a large inland body of water on the northwestern edge of the Ethiopian Highlands, was first reached in 1629 by a Portuguese Jesuit missionary, Father Jerónimo Lobo, the first European to record such a visit and probably the first to stand on the shores of the source of the Blue Nile. In 1770, Scottish explorer and traveler James Bruce likewise traced the Blue Nile to its source at Lake Tana and claimed for himself the credit of being the first European to do so.

Bruce

Nonetheless, what struck Bruce most forcefully, as it had generations of Portuguese missionaries, travelers, and explorers who trod in the footsteps of ancient pilgrims, were the monumental remnants of the same Christian civilization that had intrigued Father Álvares. Some 80 miles west of Lake Tana, in the Amhara region of northern Ethiopia, lay the small town of Lalibela. A relatively unimportant settlement in the hill country of the northern Highlands, Lalibela is nowadays recognized internationally for the extraordinary rock-cut churches – 11 in all, according to UNESCO – scattered in the surrounding countryside. These structures, just a small constituent of Ethiopia's monumental heritage, have been provisionally dated to the 12th and 13th centuries and are attributed to the Zagwé Dynasty, a kingdom centered at Lalibela that was active from 900-1270.

The Lalibela rock-cut churches attest not only to the very early Christianization of the Ethiopian interior, but also to a degree of cultural accomplishment that in every respect placed the civilization responsible for their construction at the apex of economic and cultural development for the age. It goes without saying that the technical and engineering accomplishments necessary to carve a series of buildings of such substantial dimension and fine artistic detail from the hard volcanic basalt of the region are impressive.

The Zagwé Dynasty, however, for all of its magnificent accomplishments, was built on the ruins of a civilization that was older still, with its monuments and architecture more deeply buried. Those early European visitors, who encountered but fleeting evidence of this ancient culture, could do nothing more than speculate upon its origins. Father Jerónimo Lobo, who spent nine years in Ethiopia, also pictured the place in the context of the legend of King Solomon and the Queen of Sheba, remarking in his travel memoir, the *Itinerário*: "[A]nd the place where she (the Queen of Sheba) had her court still exists today, with monuments of remarkable magnificence, as well as the town where they say she was born and which still today preserves her name, the land being called Saba by the Abyssinians, all of which I saw and traversed on several occasions."[1]

James Bruce, as contemptuous of Jesuits as many other Scottish Protestants, bore a particular animosity towards Father Lobo, likely because the latter beat him to the discovery of the source of the Blue Nile by 141 years. In regards to that particular claim, for Father Jerónimo achieved a lot more besides, Bruce revealed the worth of his pen in the derision that he heaped upon it. His own Ethiopian journey was chronicled in several volumes, published in 1813, under the title *Travels to Discover the Source of the Nile*, and therein he remarks brutally upon Father Jerónimo as a groveling fanatic priest whose lies only slightly tarnished his own discovery of Lake Tana, which thereafter carried the distinction (in the British press at least) of being authentic. One can easily imagine, therefore, how poorly would be regarded Father Jerónimo's thoughts and speculations on the enigmatic antiquities that both men stood and pondered, albeit from different perspectives in time and space.

The most visible objects available for consideration by these men were the iconic Aksumite stelae, or obelisks, that had survived in a remarkable state of preservation and which stood in what was an ancient necropolis to the north of the remnant town of Aksum. Bruce suggested various potential origins for the forty or so examples that he described, concluding ultimately that what he saw and what was visible testified to only Egyptian and Ptolemaic origins. Although he offered considerable detail in terms of description and illustration, he was in the end unable to shed any light on the facts of what remained of an ancient civilization.

---

[1] Quoted: Munro-Hay, Stuart. *Aksum: An African Civilization of Late Antiquity.* (Edinburgh University Press, 1992)

Picture of stelae at Axum by Jensi S.

And in many respects, two centuries later, that is the situation as it remains today. Enormous advances have been made in archaeology and in understanding the milieu within which the Kingdom of Aksum existed, which has offered the opportunity for more fruitful and directed speculation, but the fact remains that so much of what is known and written about the Kingdom of Aksum remains largely that: speculation.

When attempting to understand the history of the kingdom, the first important aspect to take note of is its geography. If one were to consider the Tigray region of Ethiopia, the heartland of the ancient Kingdom of Aksum, one can easily begin to imagine how control of this region might have led to the rise of a great culture. The landscape itself, covering some 15,000 square miles, is arid in the north and east, but verdant in the west and southwest. The early inhabitants of this region, therefore, enjoyed conditions neither too warm and dry, nor too cool and wet, and were therefore able to establish a style of life and commerce that supported not only the basic requirements of survival, but which offered a considerable surplus. This in turn created the ideal conditions for the growth of culture, scholarship, religion, and, of course, ambition.

If trade was the natural corollary of such an increase, then the Tigray region could hardly have been better placed to exploit this. It is positioned more or less equidistant between the productive regions of sub-Saharan Africa, from South Sudan to the coast of Somalia, and that great conduit of contemporary maritime transport, the Red Sea. The principal Aksumite port of Adulis, which is today an archaeological site situated within a bay of the same name, is located on the western shore of the Red Sea, some 200 miles north of the Strait of Bab-al-Mandab and more or less at the entrance to the Gulf of Aden. This dominating position offered any power that controlled it access northward to the Gulf of Suez and the Roman world and southward to Arabia, the Persian Gulf, India, and beyond.

Further advantages of trade and position could be gained by relatively easy access to the Nile Valley, the great resources of Nubia, the seats of Kush and Meroë, and, of course, southern Egypt. Across the Red Sea lay Yemen and the southern Arabian Peninsula, and notwithstanding the ancient ties of race and culture that have naturally influenced the genetic heritage of Ethiopia, this proximity offered the opportunity to the monarchs and kings of Aksum to extend their sphere of influence east, thus gaining territory, wealth, influence and power.

A map of the region in the 6th century CE

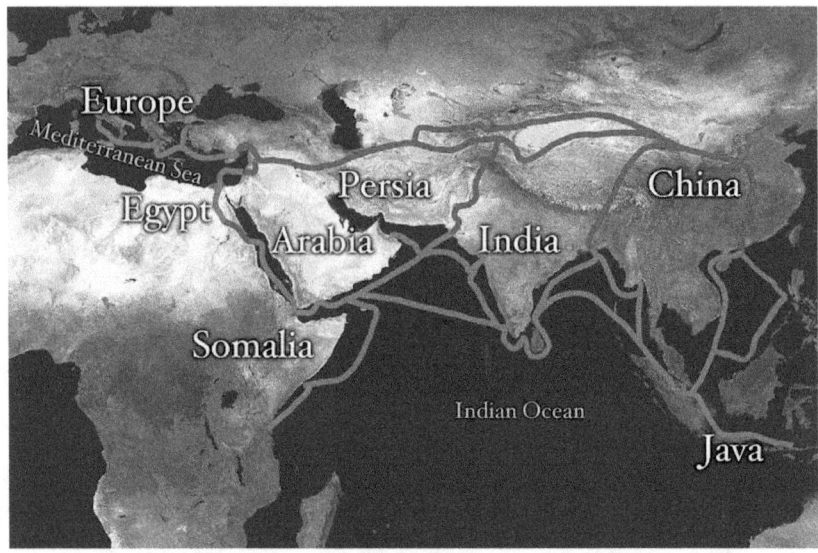

Trade routes in the region that formed the Silk Road

The Kingdom of Aksum is now understood to have been in existence from approximately 100 CE to 950 CE, encompassing the ages of Christianity and Islam, the Christianization of Rome, and the emergence of the Persian Empire. These were all events that in one way or another involved and influenced the rise and proliferation of Aksum. The Kingdom of Aksum, however, is frequently mentioned alongside the Kingdom of Kush, and indeed, Aksum is often regarded as the successor of Kush. The extent to which the two kingdoms were related by war and trade is uncertain, but they definitely overlapped in time and space, and it is quite probable, perhaps even inevitable, that the decline of Kush influenced the emergence of Aksum. Indeed, the Aksumite takeover of the Kushite capital of Meroë in 350 CE precipitated the sudden collapse of the latter.

The Kingdom of Kush centered on the region and the people of Nubia. Nubia is nowadays defined as the Nile Valley stretching more or less from Khartoum to Cairo, although the Nubian race, a Nilotic people, claims as a homeland only a narrow quadrant of modern-day Sudan (from Wadi Halfa in the north to Al Dabbah in the south). This region also serves in a historic context to define the heartland of the Kingdom of Kush. The Nubians are a dark skinned, statuesque people, whose physical characteristics attest both to their Nilotic origins and their proximity to the Dinka and other southern peoples of the Bahr el Ghazal.

The Kingdom of Kush began its rise to prominence at the beginning of the first millennium BCE based on trade in gold, ivory, incense, and iron ore alongside the opportunities for agricultural expansion offered by the alluvial soils of the Nile Valley, a long growing season, and the abundant rainfall of the period. During the period between the 16th and 11th centuries BCE, Kush existed as a colony of Egypt, ruled by an Egyptian viceroy. With a decline in Egyptian power at around 1070 BCE, however, Kush became an independent kingdom, centered on the ancient city of Napata and located on the west bank of the Nile, about 200 miles south of the present-day frontier between Egypt and Sudan.

Between 760 BCE and 656 BCE, the Kingdom of Kush rose to invade upper Egypt and for 89 years held power in what is known as the Twenty-Fifth Dynasty of Egypt. In 591 BCE, the capital of Kush was moved from Napata to Meroë. This took the focus of the kingdom away from the Nile, in part thanks to the wider availability of natural resources, but also in part because the use of the Nile as a conduit of trade had fallen into decline in favor of the overland route to the Red Sea, where Greeks had begun to establish patterns of trade and where the movement of goods to wider markets were more practical to facilitate. By the 1st and 2nd centuries CE, concurrent with the rise of Aksum, Kush had begun to fall into decline, and by the mid-6th century CE, it had effectively disappeared.

The Emergence of Aksum

The capital and center of Aksum was the city of Axum itself. Today Axum is a regional settlement, not even the capital of its province, lying on the edge of the Ethiopian Highlands and some 100 miles inland of the coast. This is a curious location for the center of a great civilization, and the fact that it does lie somewhat apart from its main historic port suggests that the original impetus for its development was not maritime. This has led to the conclusion that the first routes that supported Aksumite trade were interior, perhaps the Nile Valley, linking the emerging kingdom with Egypt through the conduit of trade with the Kingdom of Kush. In due course, however, as wider global trade links were established and maritime transport grew in importance, the location of Axum, astride the interior and the coast, proved no less advantageous. The kings of Aksum could now easily control the movement of goods between the Nile Valley, the southern regions of Sudan, the Ethiopian Highlands, and regions of Somalia to the Red Sea port of Adulis. When and under what conditions this took place remain entirely speculative, but this would certainly have marked the moment that Aksum began to develop as a major trading power and the point at which the influence and authority of Kush began to diminish.

Trade, however, comprised a comparatively small part of the wider economy, and throughout the life of the kingdom, agriculture remained the central pillar of rural life. Advantageous conditions for the development of crop production played a significant part in the emergence of the kingdom. Deep soils, optimal for the plough and requiring no additional fertility intervention, were watered by abundant rainfall, and with the advantage of a long growing season, all that was required was human ingenuity to produce an agricultural surplus. This, combined with the mechanics of trade and the potential control of both sources and markets, created the latent alchemy of greatness, requiring nothing more than a spark to ignite that inevitable flare of brilliance.

As to when and under what conditions that spark was struck, history can provide no definitive answer. One can perhaps speculate that, in common with all great empires and kingdoms of the world, the beginning was marked by the arrival on the scene of a powerful and charismatic leader who was able to harness the potential offered by serendipitous time and circumstance to forge a great empire. If this is true, then who that individual was is lost to history. It is also tempting to imagine that that flare of brilliance was immediate, and that in the obscurity of darkest Africa, an empire came into being on an impulse.

A more plausible set of circumstances, however, would likely see the emergence of one of several smaller tribal entities as primus inter pares, blessed with above average conditions of environment and leadership, which was able then to begin exerting influence over its neighbors. In this regard, it is easy to picture a social environment structured around villages, family units, and small, regional alliances gathered together under the leadership of petty chieftains or headmen. As the focus of power began increasingly to center on Axum, a system of treaties would soon emerge, reinforced by military initiative. This would in turn have gradually projected the Kingdom of Aksum into a position of regional predominance, although perhaps not for a long time gaining substantive or absolute control.

If this is true, and if it is also true that a federal structure of cohesion characterized the early Kingdom of Aksum, then this at least is somewhat supported by the historic record. Military activity was recorded in inscriptions on various surviving public monuments, and in the suppression of sundry regional rebellions, one can certainly assume the existence of vassal states that periodically sought to test the power and commitment of the central authority. This might have been during the aftermath of a succession or during foreign wars when a king's attention would have been distracted. In the existence of these vassal states, one can also assume that a system of tribute or taxation existed, and certainly there would have been some sort of an obligation toward common defense, typically, one can suppose, in the form of contributions or levies of troops.

It is perhaps worth noting in this context that hints of internal military activity against local forces loosely allied with the kingdom began to diminish as the kingdom itself matured, and from this, one can assume that the process of political development was from a federation to an absolute monarchy. This may have been the case, but frequent reference throughout the historic record to the title of "King of Kings," very much an Ethiopian standard, tends to be less indicative of celestial greatness than a paramount king presiding over a nobility of lesser, but nonetheless powerful kings.

Who were the Aksumites? Perhaps the best indication of this is to look at the modern population of Ethiopia. Today, Ethiopia comprises some 10 principal ethnic groups and an estimated 90 individual languages. Although one can assume that a variety of languages and ethnicities comprised the Kingdom of Aksum, the internal lingua franca was Ge'ez. This is described as a South-Semitic language, originating in Eritrea and entering the record not only as the official language of the Kingdom of Aksum, but also that of the court of the Solomonic Dynasty, which, claiming antecedence from the old Aksumite rulers, was a dynasty established in 950 BCE with King Menelik I that ended in 1975 with the death of the Emperor Haile Selassie I.

Emperor Haile Selassie I

The implications of this are that the Aksumites were themselves of Semitic origins, and it is indeed an accepted fact that the cultural influences of South Arabia, along with that of Cushitic speaking people on the edges of the kingdom, set the die of the future complexion of the Aksumite race. However, no statuary or portraiture survives to create a picture of what a contemporary Aksumite might have looked like, and no reliable personal descriptions have been unearthed. Images stamped into Aksumite coinage offer a small but tantalizing glimpse, and some pottery heads suggest South Arabian influences of dress and coiffure. Fragments of statues and relief sculpture from pre-Aksumite period have, paradoxically, survived better, and what these reveal is a social elite represented in the Egyptian fashion, somewhat primitive in form, and with traces of the "archaic smile." That the population of Aksum saw themselves as neither Arab nor Capoid African suggests that they recognized their individuality within the wider demographic of the region and identified themselves as separate and, in view of their use of slavery, no doubt superior.

Ancient pottery depicting the Egyptians fighting Aksumites

An Aksumite statuette

Ancient Aksumite coins

Clearly the elite of Aksumite society looked north and east for their cultural reference points, not west, and in due course, Greek would become the language of state and commerce in Aksum, at least on an equal footing with Ge'ez. Greek was the scripted language of monument and coinage, and it was the integration of Aksum into the Greco-Roman world through trade, diplomacy, and religion that marked its transition from a purely localized kingdom to an international entity. With Rome as a powerful ally and trading partner, Aksum's international status was confirmed and supported by the stable geographic, political, and historical certainties that Rome represented. This remained the case until those certainties began to crumble in the late 6th and early 7th centuries.

Aksum's connection with Rome came about through the Roman presence in Egypt, which began in earnest around 30 CE after the defeat of the Ptolemies and the absorption of Egypt into the greater Roman Empire. Relations remained within the trading and diplomatic sphere, but one might wonder why Rome chose not to extend its regional influence further south by simply assuming control of Aksum. This certainly must have been something that haunted the Aksumite rulers. Sources suggest an interest late in the reign of Nero to do so, but no clarity regarding this is available. Aksumite ambassadors are documented in Rome during the reign of Aurelian (270-275 CE), and it would only be during the reign of Diocletian (284-305) that these anxieties would have been relived with the formal establishment of the island of Elephantine, on the southern tip of the modern Aswan Dam, as the outer limit of direct Roman authority in the region.

In general, it would seem that the diplomatic relationship between Rome and Aksum was cordial and stable with just one oblique record hinting at a breach early in the 4th century CE. The story concerns the Tyrian Christian Frumentius, who would play a significant role in the Christianization of Aksum, but who for the time being arrived at the port of Adulis as a child upon a return journey from India (Ethiopia), where he had accompanied the philosopher Meropius. As it was later reported by the writer Rufinus, "It is the custom of the barbarians of these parts that, if ever the neighboring tribes should report that their treaty with the Romans is broken, all Romans found among them should be massacred. The philosopher's ship was boarded; all with himself were put to the sword. The boys were found studying under a tree and preparing their lessons, and, preserved by the mercy of the barbarians, were taken to the king. He made one of them, Aedesius, his cupbearer. Frumentius, whom he had perceived to be sagacious and prudent, he made his treasurer and secretary. Therefore they were held in great honor and affection by the king." Frumentius's introduction to the region establishes for the record the only incident of a diplomatic breach between Rome and Aksum, although no indication of what might have been the cause and nature of the dispute is offered.

Of Aksum's other international relations, it is somewhat inevitable that a strong relationship would exist between the Kingdom of Aksum and its neighbors across the Red Sea. Notwithstanding the obvious cultural influences of language, religion, art, and dress, there have been recorded military campaigns that saw Aksumite armies engaged in Yemen and briefly occupying that territory. It has even been suggested that the rebuilder of the Kaaba in Mecca in 608 CE was an Aksumite; the Quraysh tribe, who ruled Mecca, rebuilt the pre-Islamic Kaaba in that year with alternating courses of masonry and wood, and this certainly describes the generic form of Aksumite architecture. At the time of Muhammad's mission (615 CE), there was some level of recorded diplomatic engagement between Aksum and the Quraysh.

There was also an interesting political discourse between the founder of Islam and the reigning Aksumite king, or najashi (Negus), referred to by Arab historians as Ashama ibn Abjar. This took the form of Muslim political exiles entering the Kingdom of Aksum from Arabia in two waves. The first hijra, or migration, took place in 615, when a group of Muslims were advised by Muhammad to escape persecution in Mecca by seeking refuge in the court of the Ethiopian king. Emissaries were sent with gifts and representations by the Quraysh to request their return, but this request was denied, which is intriguing. The party of exiles, incidentally, included several of Muhammad's wives.

At various times thereafter, a number of notable early Muslims would seek the sanctuary and hospitality of the Ethiopian monarch, including Muhammad's daughter, Ruqayyah bint Muhammad, and it was thanks to this kindness granted to his followers that Muhammad is said to have exempted Ethiopia from the jihad, or holy war of Islam.

Some links have been suggested between Aksum and Persia, but all that is known is that ivory from Ethiopia, in addition to other commodities, were exported to Persia. Historians have further asserted that the depiction on a monumental staircase of the Apadana at Persepolis of certain figures, robed and with curly hair, were Ethiopians. Aspects of their appearance certainly seem to resemble similar statues and stone reliefs from Hawelti, a site near Aksum. According to Stuart Munro-Hay, author of what is arguably the definitive treatise on Aksumite history, "At a much later date, certain glazed wares, blue- green in color, found at Aksum and Matara, have been classified, rather vaguely, as Sassanian-Islamic or Gulf wares."

The discovery of the gold coins of the Indian Kushan Empire at the famous mountain monastery of Dabra Damo, east of Aksum in the direction of the coast, are clear evidence of some degree of commercial interaction with India, and indeed, India and Sri Lanka feature sporadically in the trade record of Aksum. There are also occasional (albeit vague) allusions to possible contacts between Aksum and the Far East, but if any such thing occurred, it is more likely that Chinese or other Far Eastern trading vessels connected with Adulis indirectly, and it is unlikely that much, if any meaningful, contact of a direct nature occurred.

Architecture and Other Expressions of Civilization and Culture

The city of Axum is described in the *Periplus Maris Erythraei* as a metropolis, and few were the centers of the ancient world that deserved or were granted this recognition.[2] All that remains of the city in its ancient form, however, are a handful of monuments. In order to gain any impression at all of the style of civic architecture peculiar to the period of Aksum, one can only consider the contemporary continuum. This is not entirely hopeless, however, because the architectural style of the region did not alter radically after the decline of Aksum, and although not much remains of Axum itself, echoes of its style and methods of construction remain very much in existence.

---

[2] The *Periplus of the Erythraean Sea* or *Periplus of the Red Sea* is a Greco-Roman *periplus*, written in Greek, describing navigation and trading opportunities from Roman Egyptian ports like Berenice along the coast of the Red Sea, and others along Northeast Africa and the Sindh and South western India. The *Erythraean Sea* implies the Eritrean Sea, which, to the ancient Greeks, included the Indian Ocean and the Persian Gulf.

Giustino's picture of typical Aksumite architecture

Damien H.R.'s picture of a church that incorporates Aksumite architecture

The city was sacked during the conquest of Abyssinia that occurred sometime between 1529 and 1543 during what is known as the Abyssinian-Adal War. This war was fought between the Christian empire of Ethiopia and a powerful local Muslim sultanate, and enormous damage was done to the monumental heritage of Axum and other sites of importance surrounding it. The city was visited prior to this event, however, by the Portuguese missionary/explorer Father Francisco Álvares, who arrived in Ethiopia in 1520 and remained in the kingdom for six years. During that time, he composed an exhaustive and detailed report entitled *Verdadeira Informação das Terras do Preste João das Indias* (*A True Relation of the Lands of Prester John of the Indies*). The text of this document has undergone numerous transformations during its history, but it offers the only firsthand observations of what remained of Axum before it was destroyed. The extract that follows was taken from the publication *Narrative of the Portuguese Embassy to Abyssinia*

During the Years 1520-1527 by Francisco Alvarez, which is essentially the same book and was published on behalf of the Hakluyt Society in 1881:

> "Above this town, there are very many stones standing up, and others on the ground, very large and beautiful, and worked with beautiful designs, among which is one raised upon another, and worked like an altar stone, except that it is of very great size and it is set in the other as if enchased (the standing stelae and its base-plate). This raised stone is 64 covados in length, and six wide; and the sides are 3 covados wide. It is very straight and well worked, made with arcades below, as far as a head made like a half moon; and the side which has this half moon is towards the south. There appear in it five nails which do not show more on account of the rust; and they are arranged like a quinas [the five dots on dice]
> …
> "This very long stone, on its south side, where the nails in the half moon are, has, at the height of man, the form of a portal carved in the stone itself, with a bolt and a lock, as if it were shut up. The stone on which it is set up is a covado thick and is well worked; it is placed on other large stones, and surrounded by other smaller stones, and no man can tell how much of it enters the other stone, or if it reaches to the ground. [Near these] there are endless other stones raised above the ground [, very beautiful] and very well worked [; it seemed as if they had been brought there to be put to use, like the others that are so big and are standing up]; some of them will be quite forty covados long, and others thirty."

The details contained in Father Álvares' report are rich and evocative, and while the account describes a city that falls somewhat short of a metropolis — in the context, for example, of Rome, Constantinople, or Alexandria — it nonetheless paints a picture of a substantial settlement. It's also apparent Axum had the optimum amenities of its age, displaying the highest standards of architecture with a significant tradition of monuments and a degree of finesse and sophistication comparable to any of the great cities of the ancient world.

What Father Álvares was specifically describing was an obelisk, or stelae (hawelt/hawelti), and the ones built by the Aksumites are peculiar indeed. Aksumite stelae are perhaps the most visible remaining emblems of a society and culture that have left tantalizingly little for posterity. The stelae of Aksum range from relatively crude stone erections to soaring and impressive sculpted towers replicating multi-story palaces. These required an enormous investment of time and resources, not to mention the high degree of skill and artistry necessary to conceive of and build them. Currently, the finest examples are found in what is known as the Northern Stelae Field, or Northern Stelae Park, in the city of Axum, wherein stand numerous carved and decorated monuments and a great many simpler, cruder forms. The largest of the stelae, the Great Stelae, is now fallen, but it was built to exceed 100 feet in height with a base measurement of over 10 by 6 feet, larger than all of the standing obelisks of Egypt. The largest example still standing is the Great Obelisk of Aksum, or King Ezana's Stelae, which now stands at the center of the Northern Stelae Park, probably the last one erected. It is over 60 feet tall, smaller than both the collapsed

Great Stelae and the better-known 80 foot tall Obelisk of Aksum.

King Ezana's Stelae

A picture of the fallen Great Stelae

Giustino's picture of smaller stelae at Axum

The Obelisk of Aksum also has an interesting history. The Ethiopian Empire was interrupted briefly by the Italian occupation of Ethiopia prior to World War II, and in keeping with the cultural imperialism of many European countries at the time, many notable historic artifacts were removed for display in metropolitan cities. This was the fate of the Obelisk of Aksum, which was found by the Italians in 1937 in a collapsed state and transported in pieces back to Italy for reassembly and display in Rome. It was officially unveiled on October 28, 1937 to commemorate the 15th anniversary of Mussolini's March on Rome. A bronze statue of the Lion of Judah, the symbol of the Ethiopian monarchy, was also removed and displayed in front of the Roma Termini railway station in Rome. In 1947, however, under the terms of a UN-brokered agreement, the Italian government agreed to return both of these monuments and other removed artifacts to the people and kingdom of Ethiopia. Although the statue of the Lion of Judah was returned in 1967, the Obelisk of Aksum remained in Rome until 2005.

Ondřej Žváček's picture of the Obelisk of Aksum

The tradition of constructing stelae was probably borrowed from the Cushitic kingdom of Meroë, and it is generally assumed now that they were erected as markers upon gravesites, with the more magnificent representing the burials of kings and the smaller representing those of the nobility or elite. However, to date, only two tombs associated with significant stelae have been identified (though further excavation at the site of the necropolis of Aksum is pending).

A picture of tombs underneath the stelae

All of the significant examples of Aksumite stelae are similarly constructed and decorated, each carved from solid sections of rock to represent multi-story buildings, with doorways and windows represented in the manner typical of Aksumite architecture. Rows of log-ends divide each story, as would have been true in a conventional building, and at their summits are rounded peaks with emplacements for iron nails that would presumably have been used to affix metal plaques of gilded bronze. These would have been embellished with the crescent and disc religious symbol of the period, with the addition of memorial imagery and relics related to the individual commemorated.

A picture of another stelae field at Axum

The material used was local nepheline syenite stone, believed to have originated in the nearby quarries of Wuchate Golo, situated to the west of Aksum. After being cut out in a rough form, they would have been transported by organized manpower to the site of their erection, where the finer carving would be completed. Erection would probably have involved the use of massive manpower and leverage in combination with earthen ramps. It has been suggested that the power of elephants might have been employed, but, again, no evidence of this exists. At the base of the decorated stelae were set similarly composed and decorated granite base plates.

It can be fairly assumed that the evolution of Aksumite stelae began with the smaller, rougher, and undressed iterations and progressed toward the more monumental and artistically accomplished forms. One must, however, take into account the material and social endowments of those creating such monuments on their own behalf. The greater the individual, the more lavish his monument, and even in the later periods, there would have been those who could aspire to only modest expressions of immortality.

Why the principal stelae were fabricated to resemble buildings up to 13 stories in height is a mystery, particularly when bearing in mind that Aksumite building conventions would never have sought to replicate that height. Similar architectural illusions appear also in nearby rock tombs and in other monumental applications.

The monumental stelae of Aksum are, for the most part, markers of burial sites, tombs, and mausoleums and are therefore indicative of Aksumite beliefs regarding death, the afterlife, religion, and of course, the relevance and value of leadership and monarchy. A variety of different examples of royal and noble interment survive, from rock-cut tombs of various types to simple, walled pit structures and more elaborate, finely crafted underground tombs. Again, the chronology is vague, but what is revealed is simply that the Aksumites, like the Egyptians and southern Arabians, were deeply concerned with the onward journey of the dead and the wellbeing of kings and notable citizens in the afterlife. Some of the best examples of funerary architecture lie beneath the most visited quarter of Aksum (what is now known as the Northern Stelae Field), and notwithstanding the monumental grandeur of what lies above, what lies below (only a portion of which has been unearthed) is perhaps of even greater interest.

In the vicinity of Aksum, and proximate to a number of stelae and other monuments, lies an interesting and accessible megalithic tomb known as the Tomb of Nefas Mawcha. It consists of a rectangular central chamber surrounded on all four sides by covered ambulatories. What is perhaps most remarkable is the single stone used to roof the central chamber, which, although broken, measures over 60 by 20 by 3 feet and weighs some 360 tons. It lies directly beneath the collapsed Great Stelae, which is what caused the collapse of the roof. Stones at either end were carefully dressed to fit and clamped with metal brackets, the holes for each of which are still visible. No entrance survives, however, since the collapse of the stelae above effectively destroyed the west end of the building and caused the rest to subside under the weight as the mass settled. This structure was clearly intended to be covered by earth as an underground tomb, and it has been dated to the 3rd century CE.

Another well-documented example of Aksumite funerary architecture is the so-called Tomb of the Brick Arches. This structure comprises four rock-cut chambers subdivided by a series of three-quarter circle or horseshoe brick arches built of fired bricks and set with lime mortar. The Tomb of the Brick Arches has the distinction of being one of very few that have not suffered wholesale robbery and looting, which means it offered a cornucopia of artefacts, including at least two skeletons, intricately carved ivory ornaments, pottery, glass fragments, and items of bronze, including decorative panels, all dated to the early to mid-4th century CE. However, what is perhaps of most interest to architectural historians is the presence of horseshoe-shaped arches, which have been recorded during earlier periods in India, tending to confirm the trade and cultural links hinted at above (although the Indian arches were carved, not built). Contemporary built examples have been catalogued in Syria, which also establishes intriguing cultural links to contemporary or earlier societies in that region.

A more typically constructed tomb is known simply as the Mausoleum. This is the largest discovered tomb attributable to Aksum, and it is entered via a monumental granite doorway carved in what might be regarded as the typical Aksumite style, with the usual architectural illusions including carved stone beam ends, replicating the combined wooden beam/stone construction typical of Aksumite civic and domestic architecture. Its plan consists of a long corridor behind the stone doorway, also entered from above by three shafts, and flanked by 10 rooms, five on each side. It was discovered in 1974, but excavation on the site was not begun until the mid-1990s. Part of the tomb was damaged at some point in history by robbers, who tunneled through about 5 feet of solid stone to gain entrance. The entrance to a second tomb was unearthed on the east side of the stelae, with a simpler doorway of rough stone topped by a granite lintel. Both of these tombs opened at one time onto a courtyard at the foot of the stelae, which appears to have been filled in with earth before the collapse of the stelae. The construction of the interior is of rough stone walling – rough perhaps being a misnomer, because notwithstanding the simple use of the material, the net effect is one of highly skilled masonry and a unique style of construction – topped with granite blocks and covered with quantities of dry stone fill. The size and grandeur of the structure is strongly suggestive of the fact that this tomb was intended to inter the individual for whom the giant stelae above was intended to honor.

Much of the excavation and a great deal of the academic material available for the study of Aksum can be credited to the work of Dr. Stuart Munro-Hay, who was the first to undertake a systematic study of Aksum and the first to work on the funerary structure described above and many others besides. It was Dr. Munro-Hay who noted, in concluding his observations on Aksumite funerary architecture in his book, *Aksum: An African Civilization of Late Antiquity*, the unexpected presence of the built horse-shoe arch structure. "These baked brick features, horseshoe shaped arches and vaults, in Aksumite buildings of the fourth century AD, may mean that our ideas about the routes of dissemination of architectural ideas in Africa, the Near East, and Spain (where the horse-shoe arch was later familiar) also need some revision. Wherever the style originated, it was certainly not expected to turn up in Aksumite Ethiopia. Without being able to assert the idea too strongly until we have more evidence, there may even be a case for proposing the brick horse-shoe arch as another Aksumite innovation, perhaps based on ideas which arrived through the trade-routes with India."

Kingship and Government

Giustino's picture of the ruins of a palace in Axum

Very little is known about the chronology of Aksumite rulers, but succession was dynastic, and government was conducted via a pyramid of authority, broadening at its base as it journeyed in the direction of the lower echelons. The oblique and vague references available hint at periods of shared rule, but in such instances, one ruler would certainly have been paramount. The power structure appears to have supported the existence of an absolute monarchy, at least during the later phases, and with such titular embellishments as "Son of the Invincible God Mahrem," it would appear that divine honors were embodied in the king and that his rule was associated with a state cult of some description, supported perhaps by a theocracy.[3]

At the point of conversion from paganism to Christianity, this emphasis on divine honor would certainly have given way to rituals of anointment and coronation. This, however, does not appear to have altered the authority of the king, who would have remained as the de facto head of the official religion, in this case the church. Kings were referred to as Nagashis, or Negus, and at times the title of negusa nagast (meaning "King of Kings") implies a paramount king preeminent among other kings, suggesting periods of federated or non-absolute monarchial authority. Other

---

[3] *Maher* or *Mahrem* was a deity associated with the Aksumites and the Himyarites. Son of main god Ashtar, and his counterpart Beher, god of the sea, Mahrem was the deity of war, comparable to Mars or Ares in Classical sources. Mahrem held a place of particular importance, and gods of the pagan period were all called the Sons of the Invincible Mahrem.

kings were grander and all-encompassing, and this was certainly true for King Ezana, the best known of Aksumite kings for his role in leading the kingdom into an age of Christian conversion. His title read, in Greek, "Aeizanas, king of the Aksumites, the Himyarites, Raeidan, the Ethiopians, the Sabaeans, Silei (Salhen), Tiyamo, the Beja, and Kasou, king of kings, son of the unconquered Ares."

In general, therefore, in the more common tradition of the King of Kings, and perhaps even under absolute monarchy, it can be surmised that the management of regions and districts was achieved through the appointment or affirmation of local rulers. From these would have been extracted tributes as a symbol of dependence, the imposition upon each to military contribution, and, of course, subjection to central military protection and authority. One inscription hints very strongly at the Aksumite political philosophy: "[T]hose who obeyed, he spared; those who resisted, he killed."

Such would have been the case with civic authority and government, but in the matter of military affairs, it can be assumed that the king would have remained at the head of the army as its commander-in-chief. Delegation of high-command responsibilities would have remained within his trusted inner circle — sons, brothers, or close relatives perhaps, with the lower command structure invested in subordinate kings, whose people would have made up the rank and file. Indeed, the organization of the Aksumite army, such as it can be determined, was regimental, with regiments tending to be associated with individual tribes and clans. Their commanders were titled nagast, which is the plural of king, implying one of many kings as opposed to the one King of Kings. Military leadership, therefore, can be construed as hereditary and dependent upon secular authority or rank of birth and title. It is possible that the rank and file of the regiments consisted of professionals, or that youth were required to devote a certain period to the service of the local king, who in turn made available troops according to predefined obligations to the King of Kings.

Military campaigns and battles were frequently depicted on stelae and other monuments, which offers a somewhat reliable insight into the formations and weapons used. Spears (both lances and shorter, close-combat variants) are depicted alongside a round shield, and items listed in the trade records of weapons imported include spears for hunting and war, as well as swords. This strongly suggests the Aksumites imported weaponry instead of relying solely on manufacturing them domestically. Iron knives, swords, and spear tips have also been found in widely scattered burial and archeological sites. It is possible that horses were in use, in which case cavalry units would have existed, perhaps as part of a professional, centralized Praetorian Guard type of royal bodyguard. Strong enough reports of elephant use exist to suggest this as a possibility, but no depictions of it have been found.

Aksumite military campaigns saw periods of control and occupation of southern Arabia, and there were periodic campaigns conducted into regions falling under the direct influence of the kingdom, likely for collecting tributes and occupying the time and energies of a standing army. No doubt there would also have been occasion to discipline errant polities and rulers, and this would have been done from time to time.

Of the intricacies of government, nothing is known, and again, it is only through the interpretation of oblique historic references that historians have been able to make theories. The chronicle of Frumentius notes that upon his capture and detainment in Aksum, he entered into an association with the monarchy that saw him rise to a position of great power both in the administration and within the structures of the emerging Christian church. It is noted, for example, that after his capture (although remaining in effect a prisoner), he rose by his intelligence, education, and application to the rank of controller of the royal exchequer and correspondence, something akin to a modern finance minister and secretary of the treasury. Under such circumstances of sophisticated government, it also stands to reason that some system of codified law would have evolved. A single reference to provisions due to the king on official visits, which appears to date to the 3rd century CE, hints only slightly at the availability of a code of regulations. Suggestions here and there of councils and committees and of advisory boards and counselors do nothing but suggest a template of government and monarchy, upon which a liberal application of conjecture is necessary to breathe life into pure probability. At the same time, it would've been virtually impossible for a kingdom such as Aksum to exist without an organized system that included ambassadors (both incoming and outgoing), messengers, interpreters and translators, scribes and clerks, assessors and collectors of taxes, and regulators of trade and market business such as currency, and weights and measures. Indeed, the sheer volume of Aksumite trade could hardly have existed on the scale that it did without law and structure. Furthermore, the eventual adoption of coinage would have been impossible without some sort of homage to a central exchange acknowledged across a vast region.

Trade and Coinage

That the king was the embodiment of the state is confirmed by the portrayal of his person on every issue of coinage, and the fact that trade underwrote the majesty of the king can hardly be more eloquently confirmed than by the simple fact of coin issue itself. Russian historian Yuri Kobishchanov, in his 1979 book *Aksum*, speculated that, in view of the area under occupation, the population of Axum could be estimated to have been in the region of half a million. Dr. Stuart Munro-Hay, commenting on this figure in his own book, concludes that no such number can reasonably be arrived at, bearing in mind the complete lack of associated data. Nonetheless, it is as good a point of reference as any, and assuming that this figure is somewhat accurate, this represents a substantial population for the time period, with an urban component associated with the city of Axum running perhaps to a few tens of thousands.

Climatic conditions are generally agreed to have been more favorable to agriculture during the period of Axum than they are now. Assuming a reasonable degree of agricultural sophistication, a surplus would have been generated, and thanks to it, the existence of large, specialized urban concentrations would have been possible. Food production remained central to Aksumite success and the Aksumite self-image, and the fact that a recurrent theme of Aksumite coinage is the depiction of an ear of barley or wheat on the reverse of every coin is clear confirmation of that fact. Famine, indeed, is first noted in Ethiopia only in the 9th century CE, toward the end of

Aksumite rule. It stands to reason, then, that among the many other exports that generated Aksumite wealth, agricultural and animal products would have featured prominently alongside the standards of gold, wildlife products, rhinoceros horn, ivory, sea turtle shell, honey, exotic timbers, and a great deal more.

Although gold, a constant of international trade, would have come piecemeal from various sources scattered around the immediate interior, the bulk of gold traded through Aksumite exchanges and ports originated in Nubia. Numerous reports support the view that gold was traded between Aksum and the regions of the declining Kingdom of Kush in exchange for such products as salt, iron, and cattle. Silver was an uncommon export, and although the issue of silver coins rather suggests local sources, it is also not inconceivable that imported supplies were used for the minting of silver coins. Copper and bronze do not appear to be locally produced, although iron existed and was produced in good quantity.

However, while base metal production, agriculture, and internal trade likely maintained the broad base of the Aksumite economy, engaging within its branches the vast majority of the city's large population, the urban elites would have been predominately engaged in trade or in associated business. Much of the responsibility of the state, and the military units that it supported, would have been directed towards the securing of ports and trade routes, and it is indeed mentioned in a handful of Arab texts that these tasks were "objects of vigilance for the Aksumite monarchy." In this regard, however, nothing but anecdotal evidence supports it.

The Aksumite Kingdom commanded not only a merchant fleet, but a military naval capacity too. Expeditions by land and sea are periodically mentioned, and certainly the mounting of expeditions across the Red Sea would have required a naval capacity of some sophistication. Likewise, the maintenance of a trading empire of the scope of Aksum could not have relied wholly on foreign fleets, so Aksum must have been home to a large number of naval and merchant crafts. Such was claimed by the 6th century historian Procopius of the shipyards of Adulis, "[A]ll the boats which are found in India and on this sea (the Red Sea) are not made in the same manner as are other ships. For neither are they smeared with pitch, nor with any other substance, nor indeed are the planks fastened together by iron nails going through and through, but they are bound together by a kind of cording."

The earliest account of trade with Ethiopia was produced by Pliny the Elder, who mentions in his writings the goods familiar to him that originated in Aethiopia. These comprised the usual litany of goods, including such staples as ivory, rhinoceros horn, hippopotamus hides, tortoise shell, monkeys, and, slaves. One compendium of ancient maritime travel and trade, *Periplus of the Erythraean Sea*, offers up just one short passage on Aksum and its main trading entrepôt of Adulis. Apart from a lengthy description of the port and location, the work mentions elephant tusk and rhinoceros horn as products of the interior and turtle shell from the coast. More lines, however, are devoted to imports, which are listed: "Barbaric unfulled cloth made in Egypt, Arsinoitic robes, spurious colored cloaks, linen, fringed mantles, several sorts of glassware, imitation murrhine ware made in Diospolis, orokhalkos, which they use for ornaments and for cutting [to serve] as money, material called 'copper cooked in honey' for cooking-pots and for cutting into armlets and anklets for women, iron used for spears both for hunting elephants and other animals and for war, axes, adzes, swords, big round drinking cups of bronze, a little money for foreigners who live there, Ladikean and Italian wine, but not much. For the king are imported: silver and gold objects made in the design of the country, cloaks of cloth, unlined garments, not of much value."

The sophistication of this consumption is remarkable, placing the elite of Aksum among the most accomplished in the civilized world. In various archaeological sites, among other luxuries, amphorae of exotic origin have been unearthed that would have been used for the import of wine and oil. Grave sites have yielded intriguing fragments of glassware from the Roman world, foreign glazed artifacts (perhaps originating in the Persian Gulf), and occasional Roman and Indian coins.

An ancient Aksumite amphora

These, however, are Aksumite imports. Exports floated the economy, and although they were often goods of a less intriguing nature, they nonetheless must have been exported in large quantities if those benefiting could afford the luxury imports that they did. From the Blemmyes of Nubia came emeralds, traded by Ethiopian merchants in India; from Sasu and Faugli came gold; from Somalia and Punt came spices, aromatics, frankincense, and camphor; from southern Sudan came the ivory, rhinoceros horn, monkeys, and precious hides, and often slaves. Salt was mined and processed in the low-lying Danakil region, east of the Highlands, and deployed as a trade good, a medium of barter and periodically an export too.

How all of this was taxed and levied can only be speculated upon, but it can be safely assumed that a sizable portion of state income was derived from taxation on trade. One can hazard a guess that taxation in kind would have been the norm, and it's possible there would have existed state granaries and depots where the collection of cereals and livestock would have taken place in lieu of taxes. Dues of a more feudal nature would perhaps have been supplied by unpaid labor, with only the major exchanges of cash and barter at a higher-level subject to a more orthodox system of taxation. The implementation of a system of coinage could have superseded a currency of a different sort, perhaps token weights of gold or other valuable metals. The use of foreign coinage, mainly Roman, helped, and other coins could have come from wherever a standardized value was acknowledged and accepted.

The introduction of a local currency, however, marked the rise of Aksum as an international trading power, for it was only among the top tier of international powers that such a thing was known. Indeed, the subject of coinage is in many respects the only aspect of Aksumite historical scholarship that is based on solid evidence, simply because Aksumite coins are the only part of the historic record that has survived in quantity. Outside of the Roman dependencies of Africa, Aksum remains the only ancient African society to issue its own national coinage. The system survived from about 270 CE, or a little later, into the early 7th century, and seems to have been in use in both external trade and internal market transactions. To what extent this monetized economy penetrated beyond the confines of the urban elite is a matter of speculation, but to date, coins has been unearthed in all of the principal archeological sites associated with the Kingdom of Aksum.

At around 520 CE, under King Kaleb, the Kingdom of Aksum entered southern Arabia, challenging the Jewish Himyrite leadership then controlling the region and persecuting Christian Aksumites. In the process, a portion of territory, part of modern Yemen, was annexed under unclear and somewhat unstable circumstances. By then, the coinage of southern Arabia was falling into decline, and the changes pursuant to this military action and to the rise of Islam reduced the energy of trade in the region and directed Aksumite attention increasingly towards the Roman world.

The Romans were by then trading aggressively in the Red Sea region, which was awash with Roman currency as a result. The gold of Rome in antiquity was a medium of trade and exchange that could be used in any situation, which indicates that the fact Aksum sought a unique currency of its own had perhaps as much to do with an expression of imperial hubris than it did the need to lubricate the mechanics of trade. The need for money spoke directly to the complexity and civilization of the kingdom, and the ability to compute, process, and execute a system of currency stood somewhat as proof of that fact. The value and weight of Aksumite currency followed the Roman/Byzantine system, and it was, for the most part, interchangeable with it. Clearly, the Kingdom of Aksum identified very directly with the Roman world by that time.

With that said, once established, the Aksumite system of currency did oil the economic wheels of the kingdom, meaning more trade and the accumulation of even greater wealth was inevitable.

As Dr. Munro-Hay remarked, "Coinage gave the economy a central emphasis from which every aspect of the state's function could spring."

With regard to the mechanics of the growth of currency use, the early issues of coinage would obviously have been limited, and a general adoption of coinage by the population would have likely been encouraged through the levying of certain taxes in currency and offering currency as a reward for products or services. Armies would be paid in coin, for example, and commodities previously expressed in multiple separate, barter-related values would be valued according to a common standard. This would eventually be widely understood and appreciated. More complex transactions could thereafter be possible across the spectrum, and the pace of trade accelerated rapidly to a pitch that brought the Kingdom of Aksum to the very zenith of its powers.

Curiously, Aksumite coins are almost absent from the archaeological record outside of Aksum, with the exception being southern Arabia. This has led historians to believe that all coinage was minted locally, and this is ascertained from both quality and method. Gold coins were typically deployed in trade, and therefore they tended to circulate mainly in trading circles, while in the wider economy, and in particular the rural areas, bronze and silver coins were more common. The language of inscription was Greek, an obvious reminder that the currency was intended to participate in trade with the Hellenized east.

Moreover, coins featured the image of the contemporary ruler as a matter of emphasis, and indeed, most of the dynastic information available comes from the study of Aksumite coins. The essential elements of design of Aksumite coins did not alter much throughout the course of their issue, although shifts in emphasis occurred, as would have been most notable when the kingdom was Christianized. This change took place during the reign of King Ezana (320=360), which allows one of very few precise determinations to be made about any event concerning Aksumite history. During and after that period, coin issues no longer displayed the crescent and disc of earlier religious observance; instead, it began to appear with the Christian cross above the head of the king. Inscriptions support this enormous cultural shift, and the issue of a coinage thus marked announced to the entire civilized world the conversion of Aksum to Christianity.

This conversion had enormous significance, because far from being a simple change of ideological direction, it was a notice of entry by the Kingdom of Aksum into a vast and growing sphere of not only religious influence, but also political and economic influence.

Religion

The conversion of the kingdom to Christianity and the establishment thereafter of Ethiopia established one of the earliest and greatest Christian kingdoms of the world, and the story of Ezana's conversion is one that harks back to Frumentius. Frumentius, or Saint Frumentius was a Syro-Phoenician Greek born in Tyre who was the Bishop of Aksum and was responsible for introducing Christianity to Ethiopia. Frumentius is highly regarded in the Coptic Church in particular, and the alliances between the Coptic and Ethiopian churches are almost too numerous to mention.

The path to conversion began with the capture of Frumentius when he was just a boy and a companion of the philosopher Meropius on a journey to the Indies, which back then referred to the Arabian world. The story is told by the monk, historian, and theologian Tyrannius Rufinus, and according to this version, Frumentius, while a prisoner, grew in the estimation of the Aksumite king, who gave him an official office. Frumentius, who was a Christian, was then offered a regency upon the succession of Ezana, since Ezana was a just a boy and too young to practically rule. From this, it can be surmised that Frumentius was probably no longer bound very sternly by the terms of his capture, and that he acquired significant power. As a result, he opened the doors of Aksum to Christian influence, encouraging the growth of Christianity throughout the kingdom. This was probably quite easy, since being Christian was part of the growing international establishment thanks to Constantine the Great's conversion of Rome to Christianity. Islam had yet to appear on the eastern horizon, and for the time being, the bonding agent of a common ideology was attractive to elites across the civilized world.

Ezana was probably converted as a child, entered power as a Christian, and duly altered the emblems of state to reflect that fact. At that point, Frumentius bid farewell to Aksum and made his way back to Rome. His route took him from Adulis to Alexandria, but there he was intercepted by the Patriarch Athanasius, to whom he related the facts of Ezana's conversion. The growth of Christianity in Ethiopia was regarded as momentous in Alexandria, and it was agreed that a See of Aksum's significance required a Bishop, so Frumentius himself was granted that appointment. Thus, he did not return to Rome as initially planned but instead returned immediately to Aksum, this time in the role of bishop. This immediately allied Aksum with the Patriarchs of Alexandra, an alliance that began a tradition of Alexandrian appointment to the bishopric of Aksum.

This Alexandrian prerogative over bishopric appointments somewhat encased Aksum within the sphere of influence of the Holy See of Saint Marks, alongside the Nubian kingdoms of Nobatia, Alodia and Makoria, and the Libyan Pentapolis.[4] From the point of view of the rulers of Aksum, the main political advantage to be gained by a bishop appointed from outside the kingdom was simply that he occupied a role more akin in the court of the king to an ambassador and could be relied upon to be indifferent to the nuances of local power. In due course, it became accepted that this appointment would be occupied by a Coptic Egyptian, which thereafter disqualified any native Ethiopian.

Having gained a foothold in the region, Christianity remained for a long time the preserve of the urban elites, monastic communities, and those living alongside major trading routes. The rural population for the most part remained loyal to animist traditions or clung to the pre-Islamic, south Arabian polytheism that influenced elite, pre-Christian faith throughout Ethiopia. It was the mission of the Nine Saints, or the Syriac Nine Saints, that popularized Christianity in Ethiopia. The Syriac Nine Saints was a missionary outreach, and though its origins are somewhat obscure, the mission entered Ethiopia during the late 5th century CE and completed the Christianization of the kingdom.

---

[4] The Seat of the Coptic Orthodox Pope of Alexandria is historically based in Alexandria, Egypt, and is commonly known as the Holy See of Saint Mark, to whom the Coptic Pope claims to be the legitimate successor.

Only three of the nine were actually Syrian, with the others having originated in Constantinople, Anatolia, and Rome, but regardless, they took the message deeper into the hinterland, and although this collision of faiths in a deeply conservative environment created difficulties, the rapid spread of Christianity in the region was achieved. The Syriac missionaries formed a nucleus of knowledge and doctrine, and many other missionaries followed suit. Thus, before Islam could gain ground in the region, a region close to the heartland of the future religion, Christianity sunk deep roots that would survive the upheavals of both jihad and communist revolutions to remain among the most robust of all spheres of Christianity.

By the beginning of the 6th century, there were Christian churches established throughout northern Ethiopia, and King Kaleb led periodic crusades against those persecuting Christians in southern Arabia, extending to Jewish groups who also engaged in anti-Christian crusades from time to time. King Kaleb's reign is also significant for the spread of Christianity among the primitive Agaw tribes of central Ethiopia and beyond.

The Decline of the Kingdom

As with many other great cultures, the factors that influenced the decline of Aksum were both external and internal. An exhaustion of the means of production through climate change, overpopulation, and over-production reduced the all-important surplus and thus stifled the creativity of a population that thereafter began to slide into cultural apathy. Such simple cause and effects as the denudation of local woodland, followed by a lack of domestic and industrial fuel, would have discouraged concentrated settlement and stimulated the dispersal of populations away from the area.

In the late 6th and early 7th centuries, hints begin to appear in the fog of Aksumite history that all was not well. Costly military adventures during the reign of Kaleb, perhaps some conspicuous reversals, and perhaps a deadening of the national spirit under the weight of the Justinian Plague, all seemed to contribute to a slow weakening of the core. The expansion of Persian influence south down the Arabian Peninsula and the occupation of Yemen, Alexandria, and Tripoli by the Sasanian Empire, would likewise have limited and circumscribed the scope of trade available to Aksum. Such trouble would then have lent encouragement to the outer constituents of the kingdom to test the cohesion of the center and create for themselves an ever more comprehensive independence. In due course, the bonding agents of empire would crumble until the edifice slowly began to disintegrate and fracture into the dust of clans and tribes. Currency would fall away as the medium of trade, monuments would tumble, and the great works of a bygone age gathered myth and legend until they subsided into the soil of almost immeasurable time. As the mighty edifice of Rome itself began to crack and fall, so its decline would slowly undermine the dependent empires that had grown so widely, and so well, under the Pax Romana.

Perhaps the final event that defined the direction of Aksum was the rise of Islam. To the east and north, the new faith drew a virtual circle around the kingdom and what was by then the Christian enclave of Ethiopia. The survival of Christianity in the kingdom can perhaps trace some of its origin to the cordiality of relations between the Aksumite king and the Prophet

Muhammad as the latter sought to establish a new faith. The Church of Ethiopia and the Coptic Church of Egypt remained the only survivors of Christianity in a hostile region, and both were for the foreseeable future isolated from contact with the core of the faith. The Holy Lands and the northern Mediterranean were abandoned by Christendom, and the great faith settled during the Middle Ages into the introspective, conservative, and self-searching institution that it became. As a result, the distant recollections of a Christian kingdom in the dark heart of Africa faded in the collective memory. The great trade routes severed, and Ethiopia languished in cultural isolation until the Age of Discovery brought Portuguese adventurers and missionaries in search of the legendary throne of Prester John.

Online Resources

Other books about ancient history by Charles River Editors

Other books about Axum on Amazon

Further Reading

Francis Anfray. Les anciens ethiopiens. Paris: Armand Colin, 1991.

Yuri M. Kobishchanov. Axum (Joseph W. Michels, editor; Lorraine T. Kapitanoff, translator). University Park, Pennsylvania: University of Pennsylvania, 1979. ISBN 0-271-00531-9

David W. Phillipson. Ancient Ethiopia. Aksum: Its antecedents and successors. London: The British Brisith Museum, 1998.

David W. Phillipson. Archaeology at Aksum, Ethiopia, 1993–7. London: British Institute in Eastern Africa, 2000. ISBN 1-872566-13-8

Stuart Munro-Hay. Aksum: An African Civilization of Late Antiquity. Edinburgh: University Press. 1991. ISBN 0-7486-0106-6 online edition

Stuart Munro-Hay. Excavations at Aksum: An account of research at the ancient Ethiopian capital directed in 1972-74 by the late Dr Nevill Chittick London: British Institute in Eastern Africa, 1989 ISBN 0-500-97008-4

Sergew Hable Sellassie. Ancient and Medieval Ethiopian History to 1270 Addis Ababa: United Printers, 1972.

African Zion, the Sacred Art of Ethiopia. New Haven: Yale University Press, 1993.

Free Books by Charles River Editors

We have brand new titles available for free most days of the week. To see which of our titles are currently free, click on this link.

Discounted Books by Charles River Editors

We have titles at a discount price of just 99 cents everyday. To see which of our titles are currently 99 cents, click on this link.

CPSIA information can be obtained
at www.ICGtesting.com
Printed in the USA
LVHW081549080920
665349LV00028B/1201